Portsmouth

a pocket miscellany

John Sadden

The
History
Press

First published 2012

The History Press
The Mill, Brimscombe Port
Stroud, Gloucestershire, GL5 2QG
www.thehistorypress.co.uk

British Library Cataloguing in Publication Data.
A catalogue record for this book is available from the British Library.

ISBN 978 0 7524 6616 3

Typesetting and origination by The History Press
Manufacturing managed by Jellyfish Print Solutions Ltd
Printed in Great Britain

Coat of Arms

A blue shield with a gold star and crescent moon has represented Portsmouth for over 700 years. Richard the Lionheart, who granted the town its first charter in 1194, had a similar design on his first great seal, which was possibly adopted from a design he saw on the Third Crusade.

*

The sea-lion and sea unicorn reflect the city's royal associations. The unicorn wears a naval crown and a representation of the medieval chain boom which stretched across the mouth of the harbour. The lion's mural crown refers to the city's former fortifications.

*

Heaven's Light Our Guide was the motto of the Order of the Star of India, and appeared on troopships. Rifles, revolvers, scimitars and daggers engraved with the inspirational message were distributed in India.

Contents

Pronunciation

Some residents pronounce it Portsmarf, Portsmuff or Portsmurf.

It means 'mouth of the port'.

The *Anglo-Saxon Chronicle*, compiled in the ninth century, states that in AD 501, 'Port and his two sons Beida and Maegla came to Britain with two ships in the place which is called Portes mutha, and killed a young British man, a very noble man'. This event probably took place near Portchester, but it is the first known appearance of the name Portsmouth in a written source.

A resident is called a Portsmuthian or Pompeyite. An Old Portmuthian is a former pupil of Portsmouth Grammar School, the city's oldest school.

Grid Reference

Ordnance Survey grid reference SU 64057 00176 (Guildhall)

Latitude 50.797611 Longitude -1.0923672

Total area of Portsmouth is 4,028 hectares, or 9,954 acres, or 15.5 square miles

Ward Snapshots

Baffins: mainly 1930s housing, includes Milton Common and Great Salterns. Baffins Farm dated back to the twelfth century: only Baffins Pond remains. Population: 15,200. Average household income: £34,700.

Central Southsea: covers residential area north of Albert Road and west of Winter Road. Largely terraced housing. Population: 14,300. Average household income: £31,200.

Charles Dickens: covers Portsea, Landport and Buckland. Areas of largely post-war social housing in area heavily bombed in the Second World War. Buckland mentioned in Domesday Book as manor of Bocheland. Includes Commercial Road, the city's main shopping area, and, hidden away, Dickens' birthplace. Population: 18,400. Average household income: £22,400.

Copnor: one of three Portsea Island villages listed in Domesday Book. Now predominantly residential, 1930s housing, but also includes substantial part North End, with earlier terraces. Population: 13,300. Average household income: £36,700.

Cosham: a village until absorbed by Portsmouth in 1920. Anglo Saxon: 'Cossa's home', mentioned in Domesday Book. Part of Wymering ('Wigmaer's people') is in this ward. Population: 14,200. Average household income: £31,700.

Drayton & Farlington: incorporated into Portsmouth in 1932, as city expanded. Drayton appears in Domesday Book ('farm near place where timber (or boats) was dragged up from river'). Farlington ('farm of dwellers in the fern wood') is free from dense housing typical of Portsea Island. Population: 13,200. Average household income: £41,100.

Eastney & Craneswater: Eastney was a small hamlet until Royal Marine Barracks were built in 1867. By the 1900s, developed and absorbed into town. Craneswater: name of a minnow pond that attracted wildfowl before Canoe Lake was built in 1886; now an affluent area. Population: 13,200. Average household income: £37,400.

Fratton: in Domesday Book as Frodintone, manor of William de Warren. Mainly Victorian terraces. Fratton Road is a secondary shopping area. Fratton Park is in Milton Ward. Population: 14,200. Average household income: £31,100.

Hilsea: was northern part of Gatcombe Manor and hamlet on old London road. Municipal boundary extended to area in 1904. Fortifications defending Portsea Island from land attack date back to Tudor times. Population: 13,700. Average household income: £34,600.

Milton: corruption of Middleton, a common next to Welder (Velder) Heath. Small village developed but swallowed up by early twentieth century. Farmland became Milton and Bransbury Parks. Largely residential, terraced housing. Population: 13,800. Average household income: £34,000.

Nelson: covers Stamshaw (dense rows late Victorian and Edwardian terraces) and Tipner (includes former naval housing, 1930s). North Tipner redevelopment planned. Population: 14,900. Average household income: £30,100.

Paulsgrove: formerly hamlet on old Southampton road, incorporated 1920. Large council estate developed after the Second World War replacing bombed city homes. Includes part of Portchester, incorporated 1932. Population: 13,900. Average household income: £32,000.

St Jude: covers Southsea Common and streets north, including Owen's late Regency terraces and villas, Palmerston Road shopping area, Victoria Road South and western end of Albert Road with its numerous bars and restaurants. Population: 11,700. Average household income: £36,000.

St Thomas: covers historic Old Portsmouth, Gunwharf Quays and post-war Somers Town estate of largely social housing, south of Winston Churchill Avenue to Elm Grove. Population: 15,200. Average household income: £32,000.

Oldest Map

Portsmouth appears on the oldest surviving route map of Great Britain, the Gough Map, which dates from around 1360 and shows 600 towns and cities, 200 rivers and all the main roads – with their length in miles. Portsmouth is labelled Portis Mouth and is represented by a single red-roofed building.

The earliest known map of the town itself dates from 1545-46 and was almost certainly made for military purposes in anticipation of a Spanish invasion. This covered the old fortified town, the rest of Portsea Island being very sparsely populated. By the end of the eighteenth century, the town was one of the best mapped in Britain.

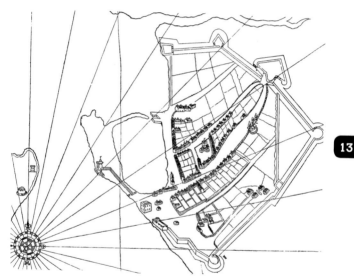

Place-names Past and Present

Beggars' Bush Furlong – extended along Commercial Road, from the north side of Prince's Street to All Saints' Church.

Devil's Acre – disapproving description of notorious area at The Hard which had forty-five licensed premises in 1896, alcohol being only one of the devil's temptations available.

Dick Leg's Alley – former name of Waterman's Alley, Portsea.

Drunken Furlong – long and narrow strip of land on the west side of Cottage Grove.

The Hard – originally the Common Hard, a cobbled hard standing projecting into the harbour used for small boats. The road facing it was renamed The Hard in 1720.

Hogmarket Street – fifteenth-century name for Warblington Street, rebuilt from stone from Warblington Castle; this was reduced to ruins in the Civil War.

Paradise View – situated at the top of East Street, Landport. There was a stinking refuse pit there which was not cleared out for at least nineteen years.

Pesthouse Field – land near the Dockyard where a pest house was erected at the time of the plague.

Point – What's the Point? Not a metaphysical question. It forms the eastern side of the narrow entrance to the harbour. Also known as Spice Island – evoking the area's involvement in the Caribbean spice trade. A notorious area of drunkenness and debauchery.

Powder House Lane – off Warblington Street, opposite Nobb's Lane. There was considerable nervousness about the storage of gunpowder in the densely populated town.

Rotten Row – an area of Portsmouth Harbour, where navy vessels awaiting repair are moored.

Squeeze Gut Alley – popular name for Messum's Court, which ran from Prospect Row to St Mary's Street. The eastern end of it was very narrow.

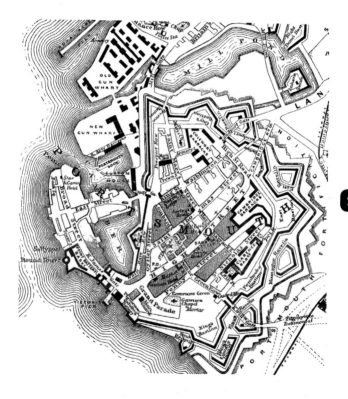

Distance From...

Place	Distance (km)	Distance (m)
Ayers Rock (named after Sir Henry Ayers, *b*. Portsea, 1821)	15,073	9,366
Baghdad	4,134	2,576
Centre of the Earth	6,371	3,958
Death Valley, California	8,513	5,290
Eiffel Tower	324	202
Gaza Strip, Palestine	3,615	2,246
Guernsey	184	115
Helmand Province, Afghanistan	5,511	3,424
Isle of Man	451	280
Jerusalem	3,632	2,257
The Kremlin	2,603	1,618
London Eye	104	65
The Moon (average)	382,500	237,674
The North Pole	6,864	4,265
Osaka, Japan	9,625	5,981
The Panama Canal	8,426	5,236
Queenstown, SA	9,562	5,942
Southampton	not far enough	
Staunton Creek, Hong Kong (named after Sir George Staunton, Orientalist and MP for Portsmouth 1832-52)	9,746	6,056
The Sun (average)	147-152 million	91.5-94.5 million
The Taj Mahal	6,975	4,334
Vatican City	1,430	889
Yellowstone National Park	7,435	4,620
Zurich	798	496

Town Twinning

Caen, France; population: 115,000; Capital of Basse-Normandie region. Caen Castle is one of the largest medieval fortresses in Western Europe. The ferry service to Caen opened up an opportunity to forge links, and in 1987 formal twinning was declared. Caen is famous for historic buildings dating from the reign of William the Conqueror, who is buried there. Portsmouth was attacked and burnt four times by the French in the fourteenth century, and in 1346 Edward III sailed from Portsmouth with a huge fleet and sacked Caen. Portsmouth was blockaded by the French in 1416 and it was during a French attack in 1545 that the *Mary Rose* sank – all in the past.

Duisburg, Germany; population: 490,000; near Dusseldorf. Boasts the largest inland port in world and is home of Konig Brewery. This link is the second oldest Anglo-German twinning, forged in 1950 as an act of reconciliation following the Second World War. As a major industrial city in the Ruhr providing material for the Nazi war machine, Duisburg was a major target and was heavily bombed. As Britain's premier naval port, Portsmouth experienced sixty-seven air raids. The spirit of reconciliation was kindled amid post-war reconstruction of the respective cities.

Sister links established with Haifa (Israel), 1963; Portsmouth (Virginia), 1982; Sydney (Australia), 1984; and Maizuru (Japan), 1998.

Friendship links established with Lakewood (Colorado), USA, 1982; Portsmouth (New Hampshire), 1997; and Zha Lai Te Qi (China), 2004.

International Portsmouths

Portsmouth is a village in West Yorkshire, located on the A646 road in the Calderdale District near Burnley. It was originally in Lancashire before boundary changes.

There are Portsmouths in Iowa, New Hampshire, Ohio, Portland (Oregon), Rhode Island, Virginia and Michigan. A fishing village in North Carolina with the name was abandoned in 1971.

Portsmouth Village is a part of Kingston, Ontario, Canada.

Portsmouth is the second largest town in the Caribbean island of Dominica.

Portsmouth Square is a park in Chinatown, San Francisco, which is popular with homeless people and Clint Eastwood. It featured in his films *Dirty Harry* (1971) and *The Dead Pool* (1988). As well as the destitute, the square is also occupied by a statue of the Goddess of Democracy.

The combined total population of these Portsmouths is less than that of our original Portsmouth.

Southsea is a formerly industrial Welsh village on the Gwenfro River in the county borough of Wrexham.

Timeline

Alfred the Great gathers a large fleet and thrashes the Danes.

Dock enclosed by command of King John.

Siege of Portsmouth by Parliamentary forces; St Thomas's Church severely damaged.

Isambard Kingdom Brunel born in Britain Street, Portsea.

Jean de Gisors, a Norman Lord, founds the town at the mouth of the harbour.

Dry dock built by Henry VII; designated royal dockyard and garrison town.

John Pounds, disabled cobbler and Ragged School pioneer born.

Romans build a fort at Portchester.

AD 268   896   1180   1212   1495   1642   1766   1806

501   1086   1194   1265   1544   1732   1805

The Saxons, led by Port, land in the Portsmouth Harbour area.

Richard the Lionheart sells Portsmouth its first charter.

Southsea Castle finished. Henry VIII watches the *Mary Rose* sink from it the following year.

Nelson leaves George Hotel in High Street for last time.

Domesday survey records the manors of Buckland, Copnor and Fratton.

Town sacked and burned by the Barons of the Cinque Ports.

Foundation of Portsmouth Grammar School by Dr William Smith.

22

Portsmouth-born James
Callaghan becomes
Prime Minister.

Battle of
Jutland,
many local
casualties.

Portsdown Hill forts
under construction.

D-Day:
Portsmouth area
plays a major
role as base for
embarkation.

Gunwharf Quays
opens and building
of Spinnaker Tower
gets underway.

Charles Dickens
born in Mile
End Terrace,
Commercial Road.

First Public
Library
opened.

1812 1862 1883 1916 1944 1976 2001

1809 1847 1865 1910 1926 1966 1982 2008

Railway arrives
in Portsmouth.

Slum clearance.
First council
houses follow.

Tricorn Centre,
controversial
Brutalist
development,
opens.

Portsmouth
FC win the FA
Cup for the
second time.

A fashionable
new suburb,
Southsea, begins
development.

Portsmouth
becomes a city.

First horse-drawn tram.

Falklands War:
naval support
services work
around the clock.

How Many Times a Year?

...is the city visited by tourists?
7.4 million (day trips)

...does a vehicle pass the Sails of the South structure on the M275, the principal gateway into Portsmouth?
30,295,000

...does the Guildhall clock chime?
42,000

...are degrees awarded by the University of Portsmouth?
4,500

...is a word printed in *The News*?
11,268,000

...does someone borrow a book from one of the city's public libraries?
852,838 (2010, pre-cuts)

...is someone treated at Queen Alexandra Hospital Accident and Emergency Department?
40,000 (2010)

...does someone pass through the turnstile at Fratton Park?
376,800 (not including friendlies)

...does the Council receive a call related to rat infestation?
1,500-2,000

...is a kilogram (2.2lbs) of household waste refuse produced by the people of Portsmouth?
77,449,000

(All figures are approximate)

Museums and Galleries

Portsmouth City Museum and Art Gallery, Museum Road, is situated in a part of the former Clarence Barracks. Focuses on the 'Story of Portsmouth', but also houses a permanent exhibition on Arthur Conan Doyle and Sherlock Holmes, plus a decorative and fine art gallery and temporary exhibitions.

Aspex Gallery, Gunwharf Quays, is the city's leading contemporary art gallery.

Cumberland House Natural History Museum, Eastern Parade, boasts one of the few butterfly houses in the country (they fly from May to September), and also an aquarium (fish swim all year round). There are also displays on local wildlife, geology and archaeology.

Dickens' Birthplace Museum, Old Commercial Road, is furnished in style of 1809, when newly-weds John and Elizabeth Dickens set up home here.

Beam Engine House, Henderson Road, Eastney, houses classic Boulton Watt beam engines and pumps restored to original 1887 condition.

The Historic Dockyard: attractions include Nelson's HMS *Victory*, Britain's first iron-hulled, armoured warship HMS *Warrior*. Choice of museums: National Museum of the Royal Navy presents the history of the Fleet and those who manned and supported it; Action Stations showcases the modern Royal Navy with interactive displays; a new Mary Rose Museum, opening 2012, will display the hull of the *Mary Rose* together with artefacts from the wreck.

D-Day Museum, Clarence Esplanade. The story of D-Day; the centrepiece is the Overlord Embroidery, inspired by the Bayeux Tapestry.

Southsea Castle, Clarence Parade, was built 1538-44 in a key position defending the harbour entrance. Portsmouth Harbour was an active military base for 400 years; it was captured by Parliamentarian forces during Civil War.

Explosion! The Museum of Firepower at Priddy's Hard and the Royal Navy Submarine Museum are across the harbour in Gosport, accessible by a waterbus service.

The Royal Marine Museum, Eastney Esplanade, is housed in the former officers' mess of Eastney Barracks and tells the story of 'sea soldiers' from 1664 to the present day.

Royal Armouries Museum of Artillery, Fort Nelson, Portsdown Hill Road. Restored Victorian fort and home to Royal Armouries artillery collection, tracing development from pre-gunpowder siege machines to modern super-guns. Panoramic views across Meon Valley and harbour.

Portchester Castle, Church Road, Portchester. The most impressive and best-preserved of Roman 'Saxon Shore' forts, originally built in the late third century. An exhibition in the Norman keep interprets history and displays finds excavated on site.

Parks, Open Spaces and Wildlife Habitats

Portsdown Hill offers good views of Portsmouth and the harbour on a clear day. Fifty acres of south slope are chalk grassland habitat, and it is a Site of Special Scientific Interest. In recent years, better management has led to an increase in the variety of wildflowers and butterfly populations.

Hilsea Lines on the northern edge of Portsea Island. It has 80 hectares of open space including an ancient monument, defences built in 1858-71, and woodland, hedgerows, meadows, marshland, brackish lakes and coastal habitats. It is the most varied wildlife haven on Portsea Island.

Eastney Beach is on the south-eastern end of the seafront. It is a special habitat known as vegetated shingle, covered in plant life, includes naturally rare species including Sea Holly and Yellow Horned Poppy. Other sights at the eastern end include a nudist beach (populated largely by human males). The area of beach adjoining Eastney Lake is a valuable roosting and feeding site for variety of birds.

Canoe Lake opened in 1886, and was previously a fresh-water minnow pond. Despite its boating and other leisure activities, it is a habitat for Mute Swans. Large numbers of cygnets can be found there during winter.

Victoria Park, the city's oldest public park, opened in 1878 on Queen Victoria's birthday. Today, its 15 acres offers adults quiet refuge from the rampant consumerism of the city centre, as well as a pets' corner for children.

Southsea Common was used for marshalling armies and other military activity for many centuries before Portsmouth Corporation purchased it from the War Office in 1922. The site is now used for many events and is a popular place for flying kites and burning burgers on BBQs. Pembroke Gardens is at the western end.

Farlington Marshes, Site of Special Scientific Interest and Special Protection Area. With 308 acres of flower-rich grazing marsh, it is an internationally important site for migratory birds, particularly dark-bellied Brent geese – twitchers' heaven.

Portsmouth Harbour is a large estuary but has been industrialised by the Navy and supporting establishments. It includes one of the four largest expanses of tidal creeks and mudflats on the south coast. In the upper reaches, it supports nationally important numbers of wintering Brent geese, dunlin, grey plover and black-tailed godwit.

Ravelin Park is the heart of the University campus but is open for public use. On site of the seventeenth-century town fortifications, it has a nature trail and picnic area.

Baffins Pond, Tangier Road, located in a residential area, has established reed beds, and is popular for its ducks and other wildfowl.

24 Hour Timeline

Albert Road, Osborne Road and Guildhall Walk pavements strewn with unwanted kebabs and pebble-dashed by take-aways.

The first edition of *The News* rolls off the presses at Hilsea.

Commercial Road market traders set up (Thursday, Fridays and Saturdays).

First train leaves Portsmouth Harbour for Waterloo laden with City workers clutching laptops, BlackBerrys and smartphones.

Cyclists overtake traffic as the city's main roads become congested.

0230   0530   0600   0630   0815

0000   0525   0600   0625   0705

University of Portsmouth library locks its doors.

Posties arrive at Slindon Street sorting office.

Guildhall's electronic clock chimes are switched on in the Civic Offices.

Some bus services start. Minimum-wage cleaners and other early-hours workers make their way to workplaces.

The first flatulent hovercraft from Ryde hitches its skirts up onto Clarence Beach.

University and college students doing 'private study' get up to watch *Countdown*.

Table at Jamie's Italian at Gunwharf Quays? Join the queue.

Microwaves in the kitchens of the city's seven Wetherspoon's start pinging in earnest.

Shops close and queues of homeward-bound shoppers and workers form at bus stops.

The Guildhall clock chimes eleven times and then is switched off for the night.

1200   1510   1730   2100   2300

1000   1230   1600   1930   2200   2330

Victoria Park begins to fill with office workers eating *alfresco* lunches.

Vue Cinema fills with people of all ages clutching buckets of popcorn, hoping to be wowed by the latest franchised blockbusters.

Guildhall Walk fills with exuberant revellers with bare midriffs, and police officers in fluorescent waistcoats.

The decks of HMS *Warrior* and HMS *Victory* begin to fill with children pretending to be Jack Sparrow.

Commercial Road market traders pack up and a team of street cleaners descend.

Club bouncers brace themselves.

Demographics

How many people?

There are 199,100 residents (2010 estimate). Expected to rise by 1.3 per cent by 2017.The city is the second most densely populated place in the UK (after central London), and the thirteenth most densely populated place in Europe.

What's the ethnic mix?

The vast majority of the population is classed as 'White British' (86.4 per cent). Portsmouth has a rich ethnic mix with around 100 different ethnic groups and nationalities, the largest of which is the Bangladeshi community with around 2,500 people. Other minority groups include the Chinese, Vietnamese, African, Caribbean, Asian, Arab, Filipino, Indian, Kurdish, Polish, Russian and Irish.

What are the religious views?

There were 127,084 people who stated they were Christian, 4,010 Muslims, 816 Hindu, 740 Buddhist, 321 Sikh, 235 Jewish, 727 other, 37,252 'no religion' and 15,516 declined to answer (2001 Census).

How well educated is Portsmouth?

A total of 17.61 per cent of people aged between sixteen and seventy-four have a Higher National Diploma or Degree or higher qualification, while 28 per cent of people, in the same age bracket, have no qualifications (2001 census).

How many students?

The University had a total of 22,622 students in 2010, 18,356 of whom were full-time. Of the total, 84 per cent were undergraduates; the rest were postgraduate and research students.

What's the crime rate?

There were a total of 21,659 recorded crimes in 2010-11. Of these, 9,853 were of rowdy and disorderly behaviour; 3,334 of criminal damage; 3,052 of serious acquisitive crime; 123 of serious violent crime; 2,479 of assault with less serious injury; 208 serious sexual offences; 2,602 of violence against the person with injury; 1,516 domestic crimes and incidents; 595 drug seizures; eleven gun crimes; eighty-six knife crimes and no murders (2010; some classifications overlap).

Are there extremes of wealth and poverty?

The top-floor penthouse at the Gunwharf 'lipstick tower', which has an area of 4,000 sq ft, and enjoys 360° views, was valued at £4 million in 2009. From the penthouse, one can see Charles Dickens ward where 56.6 per cent of children live in poverty.

In 2008, the Portsmouth FC (former) manager's salary was doubled to £2 million a year. In contrast, one in seven people are in such low-paid jobs that they have to claim benefits to make ends meet.

A household in Drayton and Farlington gets, on average, £360 more per week in income than a household in Charles Dickens ward. Residents there live on average ten years longer than those in Buckland.

Employment

What do people do for a living?
Approximately 15 per cent in work retail/wholesale trade; 13 per cent in manufacturing; 12 per cent in real estate, renting and business; 11 per cent public administration and defence; 11 per cent health and social work; 8 per cent construction; 8 per cent education; 7 per cent transport, storage, communication; 6 per cent hotel and catering; 3 per cent financial intermediation; 1 per cent power and water supply (2001 census).

How do people get to work?
Around 57 per cent of workers travel by car, 22 per cent walk or cycle and 11 per cent use public transport (2001 census).

Who are the largest employers?
Portsmouth Royal Naval Dockyard, home to two thirds of the Royal Navy's surface ships, reportedly employs around one in ten of the city's working population.

BAE Systems, is part of the second-largest global defence company and UK's largest manufacturing-based employer and engineering company. Portsmouth sites are involved in integrated system technologies (Insyte) and surface ships at the dockyard.

The University of Portsmouth has a permanent staff of 3,000 – 1,200 academic and research and 1,800 in supporting roles.

Portsmouth Hospitals NHS Trust employs around 7,800 people (2009-10, before cuts) and is the second-largest employer. As well as doctors and nurses, a wide range of specialists, including pharmacists, physiotherapists, radiographers and speech and language therapists, and essential administrative and support services.

IBM (UK) Ltd built its UK headquarters at North Harbour in the early 1970s, on a 125-acre site of reclaimed land. They planned for between 3,500 to 7,000 jobs to be based there. In recent years jobs have been relocated overseas.

Portsmouth City Council became a unitary authority in 1997 and has 4,197 employees (3,343 full-time equivalents in 2011) delivering services that include libraries, planning, passenger transport, highways, fire, social services, leisure, waste disposal and environmental health. In addition, there are 8,663 staff members working in schools (6,406 full-time equivalents). Staffing and services are currently subject to Government cuts.

EADS Astrium, Europe's leading Space Company have 1,400 staff, who are involved in the design, building and testing of satellites locally.

Hampshire Constabulary employs 414 police officers in the city (2010-11), backed up by community support officers and other staff. The Government plans 20 per cent budget cuts.

Portsmouth Superlatives

Reputedly, the narrowest occupied domestic residence in Britain is in Manor Road, Fratton. Erected in around 1900, the frontage is 4ft 10in (147cm) wide.

The development of the IBM site on reclaimed land at North Harbour between 1967 and 1982 resulted in the largest office building in the UK (at the time).

The first centrefold to display full-frontal nudity in a magazine is believed to have been of Portsmouth-born Marilyn Cole, who also has the distinction of becoming the only British model to be *Playboy*'s Playmate of the Year.

Arguably the medication that has given the most pleasure to the most people in the world was discovered by a former pupil of Portsmouth Grammar School. In the mid-1990s, Dr Ian Osterloh discovered the drug Viagra.

In 1917, Portsmouth was the first town in the country to open clinics for the free treatment of venereal disease, according to *The Times*.

The first settlers bound for Australia embarked from Old Portsmouth in 1787 for their ships in the Solent. A chain-link sculpture, symbolising the link with Sydney, stands beside the Square Tower in Old Portsmouth.

HMS *Bounty* set sail from Portsmouth for Tahiti, under the command of Captain Bligh on the first breadfruit voyage in 1787. His mission was to pick up breadfruit plants and transport them to the West Indies in the hope that they would grow there and become a cheap source of food for slaves. It all went horribly wrong.

Jonas Hanway was born in Portsmouth in 1712. He inherited a fortune and began a career of philanthropy; he is also remembered for being the first person in England to use an umbrella.

The first density lettuce was said to have been grown by pig breeder and father of sixteen Harry Hastings, on what is now allotment land near Milton Locks.

What is believed to be the first co-operative society in Britain was set up in Portsmouth in 1796 by dockyard workers fed up with being ripped off by local tradesmen. The aim was to offer an alternative by organising and controlling the production and distribution of goods and services under a system operated by and for the people.

The first Sherlock Holmes stories were written in Southsea by Dr Arthur Conan Doyle, while he was working as a GP in Elm Grove.

Catherine of Braganza is sometimes credited with introducing tea to Britain. When she arrived at Portsmouth in 1662 to marry King Charles II, she carried a chest of tea as part of her dowry (together with the ports of Tangier and Bombay).

The first detector lock was produced in Portsmouth in 1818 by Jeremiah Chubb, who won a government competition to create an unpickable lock.

Jack the Painter, one of several names given to this arsonist, has been described as the first modern terrorist. He planted an incendiary device in the dockyard rope house in 1776 (171 years after Guy Fawkes' Gunpowder Plot). He was hanged from the highest gibbet ever used in Britain, 65ft above the dockyard gates.

It has been suggested that the first rock-and-roll gig in Britain took place in the New Theatre Royal. Tony Crombie and his Rockets appeared on 10 September 1956.

HMS *Warrior*, berthed on a jetty beside the dockyard, was launched in 1860, and was Britain's first iron-hulled, armoured warship, and the largest warship in the world at 9,210 tons.

Eponymous Portsmouth

The Portsmouth Yardstick is a system of handicapping used in dinghy, small keelboat and multi-hull racing.

The Portsmouth ball-valve is the most common type of valve used in toilet cisterns, having largely replaced the inferior, and noisier, Croydon ball-valve.

The Portsmouth Road was a historic road linking London with the country's major naval port. Towns and villages on the road developed and thrived as a result. The modern A3 largely follows its route.

The Portsmouth Defence is the name of a defence in a murder case, whereby an accused person claims the victim made a provocative gay advance that made the defendant lose control and kill the victim.

The first Portsmouth Treaty (1905) was signed in Kittery, Maine near Portsmouth, New Hampshire, ending the Russo-Japanese War.

The second Portsmouth Treaty (1948) was signed aboard HMS *Victory* in the Dockyard, which committed Britain to withdrawing troops from Palestine.

The Portsmouth Sinfonia, branded 'the world's worst orchestra', was formed at the Portsmouth College of Art in 1970. The orchestra recorded several albums, performed in the Albert Hall and had a top 40 single with their 'Classical Muddly'.

Portsmouth is the name of an annoying, traditional folk song, revived in 1976 by *Tubular Bells* composer Mike Oldfield.

Portsmouth Point is an overture for orchestra composed by William Walton in 1925 and inspired by Thomas Rowlandson's famous print which is reproduced as a mural on The Bridge Tavern on the Camber.

What they said about Portsmouth

'The towne of Portesmuth is murid (walled) from the est tour a forowgh (furrow) length with a muddle waulle armid with tymbre, wher on be great peaces both of yren and brazen ordinauns, and this peace of the waulle having a diche without it rennith so far flat south south est, and is the place most apte to defende the town ther open on the haven...the toun of Portesmouth is bare and little occupied in time of pece.'
John Leland, *c.* **1540**

'A poor beggarly place, where is neither money, lodging nor meat.'
Sir George Blundell, 1627

'...and I walked...to the Dock and saw all the Stores, and much pleased with the sight of the place.'
Samuel Pepys, 1661

'...a very good town well built with Brick and Stone its not a large town, there are Walls and Gates about it and at least eight Bridges and Gates without one another with Ditches which secures it very strongly to the Landward; to the Sea the fortifications are not so strong, there is a platform with Guns and Pallisadoes (and) a good dock for building shipps...'
Celia Fiennes, *c.***1690**

Mens cujusque is est Quisque.

SAM·PEPYS·CAR·ET·IAC·ANGL·REGIB·
A SECRETIS ADMIRALIÆ.

R·W· sculp

' ...it is chosen, as may well be said, for the best security to the navy above all the places in Britain... besides its being a fortification, is a well inhabited, thriving, prosperous corporation; and hath greatly enrich'd of late by the fleet's having so often and so long lain there'
Daniel Defoe, 1724

'I inspected the fortifications there, which are in good repair....the Dockyard, or the place where ships are built, is of an enormous size and has a great many splendid buildings. But I couldn't go there, because I was a foreigner.'
Joseph Haydn, 1794

'The ramparts are planted, and used by the inhabitants as an agreeable lounge and promenade, and afford ever varying views of the shipping and surrounding scenery... on the beach is an extensive bathing establishment called the King's Rooms, with warm, cold and medicated baths, Promenade and Assembly rooms.'
J.M.W. Turner, 1849

'On leaving the Station I was first struck by the poorness of the streets, the quantity of timber yards, and tricycles and the scarcity of soldiers and sailors, however the last have become plentiful... After wanderings in a Fly we finally settled at the Queen's Hotel which seems comfortable, a queer old house with mountainous floors...'
Beatrix Potter, 1884

'Seedy at times, grim in places, but colourful and tinted with the hues of history.'
John Arlott, cricket commentator and author, 1969

What they said about Portsmouth People

'...its inhabitants are living proofs that it is unexceptionally one of the healthiest towns in all England. Its air is salubrious – its ground fertile – and its contiguity to the sea renders it alike favourable to health, commerce or recreation.'
Portsmouth Guidebook, 1792

'...crowded with a class of low and abandoned beings, who seem to have declared open war against every habit of common decency... The riotous, drunken, and immoral scenes of this place, perhaps, exceed all others... here hordes of profligate females are seen reeling in drunkenness, or playing upon the streets in open day.' **Dr George Pinckard, 1795**

'...the island setting gives it a unique sense of definition; it really is a place apart... Pompey is uncursed by money. People often struggle to get by. Whole areas are increasingly blighted by family breakdown, substance abuse, petty crime and grinding poverty. At the same time there's a resilience and rough wit about Pompey families that can make living in the city a very warm and rewarding experience.' **Graham Hurley, 2011**

'I appeared on a stage three times and died a bloody death. I could hear myself walk off the stage.'
Spike Milligan, bemoaning Portsmouth on *Room 101*, 1999

'If Portsmouth wasn't there the South Coast would fray around the edges... people in Southsea would just fall into the sea.'
Paul Merton defending Portsmouth against Spike Milligan on *Room 101*, 1999

'There's no beer, no prostitutes and people shoot at us. It's more like Portsmouth.'
A British soldier in response to Defence Secretary Geoff Hoon, who compared an Iraqi city with Southampton.

'One of the most depressed towns in southern England, a place that is arguably too full of drugs, obesity, underachievement and Labour MPs.'
Boris Johnson, 2007

Spinnaker Tower

At 557ft high (170m), it is the tallest accessible structure in UK outside London.

Its design represents a spinnaker sail billowing in the wind, reflecting its maritime location.

The total amount of concrete used in construction would fill five-and-a-half Olympic-sized swimming pools.

The total length of the eighty-four piles used is over 2 miles.

One pile was driven 164ft into the ground, the equivalent of the height of Nelson's Column.

The length of steel reinforcing the shafts and decks is 125 miles.

The bows are formed from 1,200 tonnes of structural steel.

The bows were made by the same company that produced HMS *Warrior's* deck beams in 1860.

The glass in the observation decks is 4cm thick and supported by special fins and stainless steel posts.

The 27m spire weighs 14 tonnes.

In high winds the tower can flex 6in (150mm).

The tower was painted with 4,000 litres of white paint at a cost of £300,000.

The tower, due to be open for millennium night, was finally opened on 18 October 2005, 1,751 days late.

The panoramic glass lift was made in Italy and is designed to carry sixteen passengers at approximately 1.6m/sec, reaching the first viewing deck in approximately seventy seconds. It has never worked.

Construction went over budget, with an overall cost of £35.6 million.

The tower is said to have a 'design life' of eighty years.

Notable buildings

The Guildhall, originally built 1886-90, cost £137,098 (and two builders' lives). Its grandeur was intended to convey civic pride. Described as 'styled in lumbering classicism', it was rebuilt after wartime bombing to a less elegant design, losing its tall cupola.

The Cathedral Church of St Thomas, Old Portsmouth, was originally founded in 1188. The choir and transepts survive from the medieval church. The present tower dates from 1685-91 and the cupola from 1703. It became a cathedral in 1927; the nave was added in 1990-91.

Royal Garrison Church, Old Portsmouth. Originally part of Domus Dei (God's house) or Hospital of St Nicholas, the building serving as an almshouse and hospice for travellers for over three centuries. It was restored in 1867-68 and became the Garrison Church. Bombed in 1941, the nave has remained roofless since.

The Round Tower was completed in around 1418. A huge iron chain was linked to a similar tower on the Gosport side in 1522 in an attempt to block enemy ships. Nearby Square Tower was built in around 1494.

Southsea Castle was built 1538-44, probably to a design by Henry VIII; it was extended by earthen ramparts in the 1860s.

Wymering Manor is said to be the oldest building in the city, having been recorded in the Domesday Book of 1086, though most of current building dates from the sixteenth or seventeenth century (private property).

Fort Cumberland was built in the 1740s to defend the entrance to Langstone Harbour. It is described as 'the most important surviving example of an eighteenth century star fortress in Britain' (pre-booked tours only).

Buckingham House, 11 High Street, possibly dates from Tudor times. By the seventeenth century, it was an inn called The Spotted Dog, later named after an unpopular duke who was murdered here. It was home to Dr William Smith; physician to the garrison and founder of Portsmouth Grammar School in the early eighteenth century (private property).

Quebec House, Bath Square, is a weatherboarded house, built in 1754 as a bathing house where customers benefited from immersion in seawater from harbour (private property).

Palmerston's Folly is the name given to the forts built as part of an extensive ring of fortification, prompted by fear of French attack and initiated by Prime Minister Lord Palmerston in 1859. Four sea forts were built in the Solent: Spitbank, No Man's Land, Horse Sands and St Helen's. Five were built along Portsdown Hill as defence against landward attack: Forts, Wallington, Nelson, Southwick, Widley and Purbrook. The line was finished off at eastern end with Crookhorn Redoubt and Farlington Redoubt, with Fort Fareham in the west. By the time of completion in 1880, the threat had receded.

Portchester Castle, the most impressive and best-preserved of the Roman 'Saxon Shore' forts, originally built in the third century; the Norman castle being built in the north-west corner of a Roman fortress. Military importance declined in fourteenth century as the upper reaches of the harbour silted up.

St Jude's Church, Kent Road, was built in 1851 by developer Thomas Ellis Owen as a marketing tool to attract buyers for his up-market terraces and villas.

St Mary's Church, Fratton Road. A medieval church stood on this site but was briefly replaced by another designed by Thomas Ellis Owen, finished in 1843. Perpendicular in style, the current 1887-89 replacement, designed by Sir Arthur Blomfield, was described as 'architecturally splendid if not quite outstanding' by Pevsner.

The New Theatre Royal was redesigned in 1900 by Frank Matcham. In the 1960s, the Council gave permission for demolition, but conservationists campaigned and preserved it.

Tourism

Around 68 per cent of visitors arrive by car (or van/motorcycle), 9 per cent by ferry, 9 per cent by train, 8 per cent by bus or coach, 4 per cent visit on coach tours and 1 per cent on foot.

It is estimated that about 7.4 million tourist day-trips were made to Portsmouth in 2008; just over a third involved day trips to Gun Wharf Quays.

Annual number of visitors to top attractions:
Historic Dockyard: 532,158 (2009)
Spinnaker Tower: 292,000 (2010)
City Museum & Art Gallery: 97,195 (2010/11)
Royal Armouries, Fort Nelson: 76,715 (2008)
Cumberland House Natural History Museum: 70,429 (2010/11)
Portsmouth Cathedral: 68,952 (2008)
D-Day Museum: 57,895 (2010/11)
Royal Marine Museum: 48,615 (2009/10)
Southsea Castle: 26,210 (2010/11)
Charles Dickens' Birthplace Museum: 4,309 (2010/11)
Eastney Beam Engine House: 1,610 (2010/11)

In total, around £375,569,000 was spent on trips to Portsmouth in 2008 by staying and day visitors.

This income to the local economy is estimated to have supported around 7,464 full-time equivalent jobs and 10,142 actual jobs (with the addition of seasonal and part-time employment).

The top ten 'features or images' most associated with Portsmouth identified in a survey of 501 visitors to Portsmouth were:

35 per cent, Spinnaker Tower; 19 per cent, Royal Navy; 18 per cent, boats or ships; 17 per cent, Gunwharf Quays; 16 per cent, the sea; 15 per cent, the Historic Dockyard; 14 per cent, the seafront; 13 per cent, HMS *Victory*; 13 per cent, shopping; 6 per cent, ferry (presumably to go on to elsewhere).

HMS *Victory* facts

HMS *Victory* is still in commission as the flagship of the Second Sea Lord and is the oldest commissioned warship in the world. She was dry-docked in 1922. Her anchor is displayed on Clarence Parade as a Trafalgar memorial, close to the hovercraft terminal.

Built at Chatham Dockyard, the keel was laid in 1759 but the ship was not completed until 1765.

Approximately 6,000 trees were used in her construction. The oak used in the underwater planking came from Poland and East Prussia and is 2ft thick at the waterline.

30,000 cubic ft of oak from Hampshire, Sussex and Kent forests had been seasoned for about thirteen years.

She cost a total of £63,176 and 3*s* to build (about £7 million today, using RPI).

A previous HMS *Victory* had sunk with all hands in 1744, so there was some trepidation about reusing the name.

Of a complement of 850 officers and men, twenty-two were Americans.

The ship had forty powder monkeys, one of whom was a woman in disguise who was married to a Maltese sailor serving on board.

The youngest crew member was John Doag of Edinburgh, aged ten years. Some powder monkeys in the Navy were as young as six.

Sea-going stores included 50 tons of beer, 45 tons of ship's biscuit, 300 tons of water and 30 tons of salt beef and pork.

A seaman's daily ration included 8 pints of beer, 2 pints of wine or half a pint of rum.

In 1878, William Gilbert, of Gilbert and Sullivan, made sketches of HMS *Victory* in Portsmouth Harbour to use as a basis of their sets for the comic opera HMS *Pinafore*.

Dockyard trivia

The chief executive of Portsmouth Naval Base Property Trust is a Mr Goodship.

In 1638, the Master Shipwright of Portsmouth Dockyard was a Mr Boate.

The first dry dock in the world was built in Portsmouth in 1495-96 by Sir Reginald Bray during the reign of Henry VII.

The first known warships to be launched were the *Sweepstake* and the *Mary Fortune* in 1497. The *Sweepstake* was renamed the *Katherine Pomegranate* in 1511.

Reputedly the longest building in the world (at the time) was built in the dockyard in 1776. The Ropery was 1,095ft long.

The architect and civil-engineer Thomas Telford's first architectural design was a row of houses for dockyard workers, Short Row, built in 1787.

In 1802, the world's first steam dredger was launched, having been designed and built in Portsmouth by Sir Samuel Bentham and engineer Simon Goodrich.

The age of mass production using metal machine tools was said to have started in the Dockyard in 1809 when Marc Isambard Brunel introduced the production of rigging pulley blocks.

The first modern battleship, the *Dreadnought*, was built and the city became known as the cradle of the Dreadnoughts.

The first oil-fired battleship, HMS *Queen Elizabeth*, was launched in 1913.

The aircraft carrier HMS *Queen Elizabeth*, currently under construction in Portsmouth, will be, with its sister carrier HMS *Prince of Wales*, the largest ship ever built for the Royal Navy. Due for service in 2020, the budget for both ships is £3.8 billion. The combined cost of the first two warships built at Portsmouth in 1497 was £230.

Portsmouth Port

Portsmouth is one of the largest fruit-handling ports in the country and processes:

100 per cent of the UK's Jersey potatoes.

65-70 per cent of the UK's bananas (Dole, Fyffes, Geest).

100 per cent of the UK's Moroccan citrus fruits.

Annual imports (in 2010) totalled 828,324 tonnes on 244 ships, over 70 per cent of which was fruit from Belize, Costa Rica, Agadir, Columbia, the Dominican Republic and the Windward Islands.

Exports totalled 84,846 tonnes on eighty-one ships.

Passengers and vehicles (2009/10)
The Isle of Wight Car Ferry carried 948,572 vehicles and 2,446,901 passengers.

The Isle of Wight Passenger Ferry carried 1,378,370 passengers.

The Hovercraft carried 849,150 passengers (2009).

The Gosport Ferry carried 3,392,471 passengers.

The Continental and Channel Island Service carried 692,848 vehicles, 256,842 freight vehicles and 2,288,363 passengers.

Historic Odd Jobs

Mudlarks: Originally scavengers, picking up old rope and whatever the tide brought in at Portsea. In the late nineteenth century, they diversified into entertaining holidaymakers as they arrived by steamer or train. Boys, and some girls, would dive into the mud or water for coins tossed from the pier. They were regularly chased away by police who thought them no better than beggars.

Prostitutes: Estimates of the number of prostitutes working in the port and garrison town at the end of the eighteenth century vary between 2,000 and 20,000. Many of them carried out their trade openly on the street, much to the shock of visitors. At that time, large numbers of seamen were confined to their ships when in port to prevent desertion, and so prostitutes were ferried by local boatmen to their ships where they would be selected like cattle.

Rat catchers: In 1704, townsfolk were discouraged from soaking rats in turpentine and setting fire to them because of the stored gunpowder in the port. By the nineteenth century, rat catchers carried out their work using arsenic and dogs, and were called to the homes of both the rich and the poor, rats having no respect for status. The guardians of the local workhouse employed a rat catcher, but Portsmouth Dockyard appears to have relied on cats to keep vermin under control.

Slop sellers: not as bad as it sounds; slops is derived from the Old English sloppe, meaning a loose-fitting, shapeless garment. Basic slops for seamen were supplied by civilian slop sellers until the Admiralty introduced a uniform for ratings in 1857. Dress production, including naval tailors, was an important industry in Victorian Portsmouth, never accounting for less than 38 per cent of all manufacturing employment.

Corset makers: From the late nineteenth century many naval wives worked in this sweated trade, for many the only respectable alternative to prostitution or destitution. Thousands of women worked in noisy sweatshop conditions, hunched over their machines.

Human head traders: This trade was not, as far as is known, carried out in Portsmouth, but is included because one William Tucker, who was baptised in Portsea in 1784, became a trader in Maori heads. Tucker had been sentenced to death for theft at the age of fourteen but was reprieved and transported to Australia.

She sells sea shells on the seashore: Elizabeth Abrahams did just that at The Hard in the 1830s. Sea shells could also be used by lime burners instead of chalk or limestone.

Grave robber: In 1825, John Johnson and Henry Andrews were caught with a large and heavy trunk about to catch the London coach. They had taken receipt of it at the Star pub near The Hard, the fifth such trunk that month. The corpses in the trunks – much sought after for anatomical teaching in medical schools in the capital – had been ferried across the harbour from Haslar burial ground. The gravedigger there had discovered how neat capitalism could be – he could earn money by both burying and digging up the same dead people.

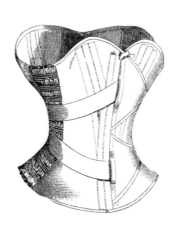

Portsmuff vernacular

Brayn split – a 'brown split' is half a pint of mild and half of bitter in a pint glass

Dinlow – a person in possession of limited common sense (derogatory)

Dockyard oyster – phlegm that has been coughed up and spat out

Dockies or Maties – dockyard workers

Gettin' off at Fratton – a euphemism for the withdrawal method of contraception, Fratton Station being the last stop before Town (Portsmouth & Southsea railway station)

The Island – the Isle of Wight

The Front – Southsea seafront

The Hill – Portsdown Hill

Scummer – an inhabitant of Southampton (derogatory)

Goin Dayn Tayn – going to Commercial Road

Lippy tower – though supposed to represent a funnel (to complement the Spinnaker Tower sail) this prestigious landmark has been renamed by locals because of its resemblance to a lipstick

Mush or Moosh – a synonym of mate or chum

Skate – sailor, also Matelot. One suggested origin for skate relates to sexual frustration at sea, desperation and the alleged attractiveness of a particular type of fish

Skatebait – females seeking sailors' attention

The Royal Navy School of Dancing – Joanna's infamous nightclub on South Parade, where skates hooked skatebait, and vice versa

Turktown – Gosport

The Yard – Dockyard

Rabbit – The story goes that wild rabbits caught on Portsea Common – enclosed within the Yard in 1864 – were permitted to be taken home by dockies. Later, it also applied to any government material that was smuggled out. A 'rabbit job' was a piece of DIY carried out in work time

Inmuster and outmuster – clocking in and out of the Yard

Seagull – a docky who is willing to work all hours

Bluejacket – sailor

Stone frigate – a naval shore establishment viz. HMS *Excellent* (Whale Island), HMS *Vernon* (Gunwharf), HMS *Nelson* (Queen Street) and HMS *Phoenix* (Stamshaw)

1964

1890s

1900s

Church Parade, Southsea Common

1920s

Portsmouth Film and TV Locations

War films: *Forever England* (1935) and *Above us the Waves* (1954), both starring John Mills; *Cockleshell Heroes* with Trevor Howard and Jose Ferrer, filmed at Eastney Barracks (1955); *Battle of the River Plate* (1956) with Peter Finch; and *Mystery Submarine* with James Robertson Justice (1963).

Musicals: *The Boyfriend* (1971) with Twiggy and The Who's rock opera *Tommy* (1975), both directed by Ken Russell. South Parade Pier famously burnt down during the filming of the latter, but it wasn't Keith Moon's fault.

Dramas: Hammer film *The Dark Light* (1951); *Time Bomb* (1953) starring Glenn Ford; *The Ship that Died of Shame* (1955) with Richard Attenborough; *Oscar and Lucinda* (1997) with Cate Blanchett and Ralph Fiennes; and the Bond film, *Tomorrow Never Dies* (1997).

Comedies: *Carry on Admiral* (1957); though it starred *Carry On* star Joan Sims, this naval comedy pre-dated the series. TV comedy: *Mr Bean: Mind the Baby* (1993); *Mr Bean: in Room 426* (1993).

Classics: Big screen version of Jane Austen's *Mansfield Park* (1999) and BBC TV version of *Persuasion* (1995).

Soaps: *Eastenders* (2001); *Making Waves* (2004), a short-lived soap at sea.

Sci-fi: *Dr Who* and his Tardis dropped in, with Jon Pertwee encountering *The Sea Devils* (1972), later fighting his deadliest enemy in *Revelation of the Daleks* (1985).

TV drama: *Casualty: Give my Love to Esme* (1997), involving a terrorist attack in the Tricorn, *Ruth Rendell Mysteries: Inspector Wexford: A Sleeping Life* (1989); *The Mouse in the Corner* (1992); *Kavanagh QC: The Burning Deck* (1996); *Silent Witness* (2004); *The Agatha Christie Hour: The Girl in the Train* (1982); *Rules of Engagement* (1989), written by local author Graham Hurley; *Going Out* (1980), a teenage drama.

Portsmouth Film and TV Trivia

Peter Sellers: comedy and character actor born in Southsea in 1925. Highlights of his film career include *I'm All Right Jack*, *The Pink Panther* films and *Being There*.

Anthony Minghella: late film director, who won an Oscar for *The English Patient*. He attended St John's College. An avid Pompey fan, he supported the team at Fratton Park when filming commitments allowed.

John Madden: film director born in Portsmouth in 1949. Television work includes *Inspector Morse* and *Prime Suspect*; films include *Mrs Brown*, *Shakespeare in Love*, *Captain Corelli's Mandolin* and *The Debt*.

Erle Osborne-Smith: of London Road, pioneering film maker, who set up the Kingston Film Studio, in 1929 (aka Portsmouth Sound Film Studios). He made *Terrors*, a fantasy featuring prehistoric monsters. The company specialised in special effects.

James Clavell: novelist, also a film director, and screenplay writer. Directed *To Sir With Love*, and wrote the screenplay of *The Great Escape* and the original version of *The Fly*. He was educated at Portsmouth Grammar School

Roy Horniman: lived in Southsea, attended Portsmouth Grammar School in the 1880s, wrote the source novel for the Ealing black comedy *Kind Hearts and Coronets*.

John Barron: played CJ in the original BBC *Reggie Perrin* series, and did not get where he got to without attending Portsmouth Grammar School in the 1930s.

Arnold Schwarzenegger: regularly stayed in Portsmouth in the late 1960s. He lived with Bob Woolger's family in Clarendon Road, and worked out in Bob's gym, now run by his daughter Diane Bennet.

Montague Love: born in Portsmouth in 1877, he attended Portsmouth Grammar School. Specialising in dastardly villain roles, he starred with Errol Flynn, Tyrone Power and Rudolph Valentino in Hollywood.

Helena Bonham Carter: great-great-granddaughter of John Bonham Carter, MP for Portsmouth in 1816-1838. Members of her family have been mayor of the town on thirty-two occasions.

Ralph and Joseph Fiennes: descendents of Edward Cecil, the 1st Viscount of Wimbledon, who served as Governor of Portsmouth from 1630-1638.

Sir John Gielgud: descended from Victorian theatrical family the Terrys. Ben Terry, the son of a publican, was baptised St Thomas's Church, in 1817. He learnt the acting trade at Portsmouth Theatre in High Street. His daughter Ellen Terry was the most famous actress of the era, and the dynasty continued with Gielgud, who was her nephew.

Stephen Weeks: made amateur films while at Portsmouth Grammar School, went on to direct *I, Monster* starring Christopher Lee and Peter Cushing; directed *Sword of the Valiant: the Legend of Sir Gawain* and the *Green Knight*, with Sean Connery and Trevor Howard.

Michael Ripper: born in Portsmouth, in 1913, and attended Portsmouth Grammar School where he loved drama. Alastair Sim, a family friend, was a regular visitor to his Alhambra Road home. When his theatrical career ended following a throat operation, he devoted himself to film and TV, appearing in over 200 films and television series.

Gerald Flood: actor whose face became familiar in TV series in the 1960s and '70s. He was born in Portsmouth, in 1927, of a naval family.

Arthur Mackey: actor in Westerns in the silent era, who was born in Portsmouth, in 1865. Appearing in over 150 films (1910-25), he also directed over sixty films.

Portsmouth authors

Charles Dickens was famously born in Mile End Terrace, Portsmouth, on 7 February 1812, and was baptised in St Mary's Church, Fratton. His family moved to Hawk (now Hawke) Street, then Wish Street (now King's Road) and returned to London in 1815. The Portsmouth Theatre in High Street (which stood on part of the site of what is now Portsmouth Grammar School) features in *Nicholas Nickleby*.

George Meredith, Victorian novelist and poet. Born in No. 73 High Street in 1828, he was the son of a tailor. He spent a miserable childhood in the town and later took to affecting vagueness about his origins.

Julia Bryant, author of a Portsmouth-based historical saga, was born in the city. Her first novel, *Waiting for the Tide*, was published in her sixtieth year following a career in nursing and bringing up a family.

Betty Burton, author of popular historical sagas, has lived in the city since the 1970s. Novels include *Goodbye Piccadilly* (1991), *The Girl Now Leaving* (1995) and *Josephine and Harriet (2004)*.

Dr Arthur Conan Doyle lived and worked as a GP at Bush Villas, Elm Grove, from 1882-1890. Business was slack, giving time to devote to writing. Amongst the novels he wrote were *A Study in Scarlet* and *The Sign of Four*, the first two Sherlock Holmes stories.

Graham Hurley – former TV scriptwriter and director, he is the author of city-based novels including crime thrillers featuring DI Joe Faraday.

Rudyard Kipling spent a miserable childhood in Southsea and boarded at Lorne Lodge, Campbell Road which he described as the 'House of Desolation'.

James Clavell was educated at Portsmouth Grammar School from 1935-40. He survived four years in a notorious Japanese POW camp, Changi, and wrote his novel *King Rat* based on his experiences. He became a bestselling author with *Tai Pan*, *Shogun*, *Noble House*, *Whirlwind* and *Gai Jin* and was also successful in the film industry.

Simon Gray, playwright and diarist, lived at South Parade as Portsmouth Grammar School boarder from 1945-47. Son of a Hayling doctor, he published five novels, forty original plays and *The Smoking Diaries*, wittily reflecting on his everyday life, decline and imminent death.

Christopher Logue, award-winning poet and writer, born in Portsmouth, in 1926, was evacuated to Bournemouth with fellow pupils at Portsmouth Grammar School on the eve of the Second World War.

Michelle Magorian, best known for her 1981 novel, *Goodnight Mr Tom*. She was born in Southsea in 1947.

Howard Brenton, playwright, was born in Portsmouth,in 1942. He wrote over forty plays including the controversial *Romans in Britain* for the National Theatre, and contributed scripts for the BBC spy drama *Spooks*.

Neil Gaiman, fantasy horror author born in Portchester, famous for *The Sandman*, is the grandson of Polish immigrant M. Gaiman, who established a grocery chain in the city.

Percy Westerman, children's writer, was born in Portsmouth in 1876, and was educated Portsmouth Grammar School. He wrote over 170 *Boy's Own* type adventure yarns that enthralled several generations.

Olivia Manning, born at No.134 Laburnum Grove, in 1908, was most famous for her trilogies collectively known as the *Fortunes of War*.

Nevil Shute, author of many popular novels, including *A Town Like Alice* (1950) and *On the Beach* (1957). He brought his company Airspeed Ltd to Portsmouth, 1931 and lived in Helena Road.

Walter Besant, Victorian novelist and historian, was born in Portsmouth, in 1836. Like Dickens, he drew attention to the plight of the urban poor.

James Riordan, born in Portsmouth, was a professor of Russian Studies and a successful children's author. His novel *Sweet Clarinet* was shortlisted for the Whitbread (now Costa) book award in 1998.

Lilian Harry, prolific author of historical sagas, born in Gosport, worked at Telephone House, Elm Grove, before taking up writing. She also writes under the name Donna Baker.

H.G. Wells was bored rigid during the two years he spent as apprentice at Hide's Drapery Store, King's Road. He later recalled that the period 1881-83 was 'the most unhappy hopeless period of my life'. Drapers' stores figure in several of Wells' novels, including *Kipps* (1905) and *The History of Mr Polly* (1910).

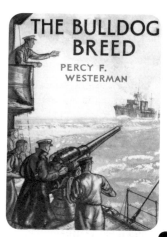

Blue plaques

English Heritage has put up seven plaques:

Lieutenant Norman Holbrook VC (1888-1976). Submariner, hero of Dardenelles, educated at Portsmouth Grammar School. Plaque on wall of home Warleigh, Grove Road South, part of St John's College.

Fred T. Jane (1865-1916). Naval author (*Jane's Fighting Ships*), artist, propagandist. Lived at No.17 Elphinstone Road from 1898-1911. (Also a City Council plaque on a block of flats on the corner of Clarence Parade and Palmerston Road, the site of another residence.)

Rudyard Kipling (1865-1936). Writer and Nobel Laureate lived at No.4 Campbell Road, Southsea as a boy, 1871-77.

Thomas Ellis Owen (1804-1862). Architect, developer of Southsea. Lived in house now occupied by Portsmouth High School for Girls, Dovercourt, Kent Road, Southsea, from 1849.

Peter Sellars (1925-1980). Comedy and character actor, born in flat above 'Postcard Corner', now Mayflower Chinese Restaurant, No.96 Castle Road, Southsea.

Commander Edwin Unwin VC (1864-1950). Hero of Gallipoli. Lived at No.12 Helena Road, Southsea (next door, No.14, was home of author Nevil Shute, commemorated with a City Council plaque).

Dame Francis A. Yates (1899-1981). Renaissance historian, born at No.53 Victoria Road North, Southsea.

The City Council has also put up plaques that include:

Sir Alec Rose, round-the-world yachtsman (Hovercraft terminal on Clarence Parade).

W.L Wyllie, marine artist (Tower House, Old Portsmouth).

John Pounds, philanthropist, inspiration for the ragged school movement (Memorial Church, High Street).

Thomas Telford, civil engineer, worked in Portsmouth Naval dockyard from 1784-1786 (Storehouse No.9, HM Dockyard).

Viscount Montgomery of Alamein, Commander of the 8th Army and war hero (Ravelin House, Ravelin Park, where he lived as Garrison Commander, 1937-38).

Sir Arthur Conan Doyle, creator of Sherlock Holmes (Bush House, Elm Grove).

Portsmouth Football Club, celebrates its foundation in 1898 at No.12 High Street.

Seasons

Pompey by Name

The nickname Pompey refers to Portsmouth Football club or to the city itself. The first use referenced by the *Oxford English Dictionary* dates from 1899, but its origins are uncertain. The following have been suggested:

A eighty-gun French warship *Le Pompee*, captured in 1793, which was based in Portsmouth Harbour for many years.

A drunken sailor fell asleep at a talk on the Roman Empire by Agnes Weston, the famous naval temperance worker. Roused from a beery slumber he heard that the general, Pompey, had been killed, and shouted out, 'Poor old Pompey!' The cry was repeated at Pompey matches.

In 1781, some Portsmouth-based English sailors scaled the 98ft-high Pompey's Pillar near Alexandria, toasted their ascent in punch and became known as 'The Pompey Boys'.

Sailors used the abbreviation 'Pom. P.' in ships' logs, an abbreviation of Portsmouth Point.

Pompey Trivia

Pompey's fans include TV hosts Fred Dinenage, Tommy Boyd, Mick Robertson, Sky Sports' Ian Darke, Foreigner frontman Mick Jones and Jon Cruddas MP.

While directing *The English Patient* in the North-African desert, film director Anthony Minghella had the *Football Mail* delivered to him every week.

The first ever league game to be played under floodlights took place on 22 February 1956 between Portsmouth and Newcastle United. Pompey lost 2-0.

'One only has to be in Portsmouth five minutes to discover that football dominates people's thoughts and conversation. Even the general election was said to have taken second place. Moreover it concerns the ladies no less than their menfolk. It was a female voice which pooh-poohed the prospect of a Portsmouth game ever being televised. "There must," she said, 'be better music-hall acts in the country."' *The Times*, 1959

The 1966 World Cup winning England manager Sir Alf Ramsey once (briefly) considered managing Pompey. A 1974 headline read, 'Sir Alf could ring in the good times again'. He didn't.

Avram Grant's tenure as manager, or 'Director of Football', in 2009-10, reportedly prompted his wife to comment on her husband's fondness for brothels: 'He's the manager of Portsmouth. Do you know how tough that is? He's a great manager stuck in a crappy team. He works so hard, he needs two massages a day, and from two women, not one.'

Fratton Park is 'Krap Nottarf' backwards.

'Visiting the lavatory is a life-threatening experience.' Comment on Fratton Park, The *Independent*, 2004

'Watching Portsmouth is a bit like living with the possibility of overwhelming moments of pleasure and the absolute guarantee of pain.' The *Independent*, 2008

Portsmouth Characters

Ebenezer Breach, a Landport man, was an advocate of the idea that the earth was flat, publishing pamphlets and giving talks on his theory. In 1893, he addressed a packed Albert Hall in Southsea with a hand-crafted model of the flat earth. The audience rioted, and someone wrenched the North Pole from the centre of the model. Chairs and tables were overturned and manuscripts and pamphlets were scattered over the floor. The model was thrown around the hall and beaten to pieces with sticks. Mr Breach escaped out of a back door with the North Pole under his arm.

Billy Baker was one of John Pounds' last ragged scholars, a street urchin who had been discovered asleep and wrapped up on the doorstep of a baker's shop in Broad Street. When he was old enough he delivered newspapers and ran errands for a few coppers which would pay for a supper from a fried fish shop and a night in the attic of the Tower Lane Doss House (known as the 'Needies Palace'). He often shared his meagre earnings and scraps of food with other homeless children who slept in Piper's Alley, at the Arches or in Cockle's Yard, in a small way perpetuating John Pounds' philanthropy.

Lord Charles Beresford was a Victorian action man with careers as an admiral and a MP for Portsmouth from 1910-16. A passionate self-publicist, he attempted to embody the John Bull spirit, travelling with a bulldog to reinforce a patriotic image. The Prince of Wales' mistress, the Countess of Warwick, fell for him and they began an affair. At a house party, late one night, Beresford crept into what he thought was her bedroom and leapt on to the bed whooping 'cock-a-doodle-do!' Following some frantic fumbling a lamp was lit and Beresford found himself lying between the Bishop of Chester and his wife.

Pompey Lil was a well-known prostitute who worked in Portsea in the early to mid-twentieth century. She was said to have had no teeth and a false eye, but was 'ever so nice' and 'well spoken'. Other local street women were Lancaster Lil, Irish Pat, Irish Peggy, Big Jean and Scots Maggie.

Marty 'Docker' Hughes stood as a candidate in the 1987 General Election representing the notorious '6.57 crew' of Pompey-supporting thugs. His demands included duty-free booze on the Gosport ferry, a racecourse on Southsea Common, the requirement that magistrates should have served time in prison and the building of a wall around Southampton to contain its inhabitants. The 455 votes he received skewed the election result and handed the seat to the Conservatives.

Dick King lived in Bath Square and was described as 'the uncrowned king of Point'. He was 6ft 3in, broad and strong, and ran the fish market in Station Road. When in a good mood, he threw half-sovereigns to poor children, but had a foul temper when drunk. In the early 1900s, he was drinking in the Star and Garter pub in Broad Street, close to where the horse trams terminated. His mates wagered that he couldn't push a tram into the sea. So he did.

Jim Sunshine, who lived in Oyster Street in a dilapidated cottage with only half a roof, was an odd-job man (who didn't bring his work home). He was reputed to have saved forty-eight people from drowning in the harbour and from house fires.

Main Roads a Century Ago

Commercial Road

High Street

Ghostly Goings-on

Admiral Collingwood Inn – A naval officer unaccountably found a young sailor in his room. Right.

Broad Street – the site of the Blue Posts Inn is said to be haunted by a bushy-whiskered, head-bandaged sailor, killed after being hit over the head with a pewter pot in a fight with marines over prostitutes in the eighteenth century.

Buckingham House, High Street – haunted by the sounds of murder and the ghost of a man in seventeenth-century clothing dashing out of one of the rooms. Research establishing that the Duke of Buckingham was murdered in this house in 1628 has lent credence to this story.

Clarence Pier – ghost of John Felton, local hero who killed the Duke of Buckingham, is said to haunt the pier, close to where his body was displayed after execution at Tyburn.

Fort Cumberland – ghost of a French spy, hanged in the square outside the Commander's lodgings during the Napoleonic Wars.

Fort Nelson – ghost of a soldier, found drunk on duty. He was court-martialled but committed suicide before he could be punished.

Fort Purbrook – ghost of a red-coated sergeant.

Fort Widley – ghostly drummer boy, spirits of French Napoleonic soldiers and an elderly lady.

King's Bastion – haunt of bearded sailors and women in grey.

King's Theatre – a man in brown, possibly the ghost of an act that died on stage. Boom boom.

Theatre Royal – ghost of an actor-manager, said to have shot himself in a dressing room.

Portsmouth Harbour – said to be haunted by Jack the Painter, executed in 1776 for starting a fire in the Dockyard. Rattles his chains in a high wind, unhindered by the fact that he was disembowelled.

Quebec House, Old Portsmouth – ghost of Captain Seton, Britain's last duellist in 1845, perhaps reviewing his tactics.

The Registry pub, St Michael's Road – ghost of a gentleman dressed in stovepipe hat, long grey coat with carved stick, believed to be a beadle connected with the building's former function as workhouse offices.

Royal Marine Museum (Eastney Barracks) – a small child, the daughter of a soldier, killed when run over by a horse and carriage. Also an officer, let down in love, who allegedly shot himself after burning some love letters. The smell of burnt letters is said to haunt the attic.

St Mary's Street – an athletic ghost, Springheeled Jack, is said to have frequented the churchyard. He jumped over walls and hedges to frighten spooning couples at night. Pervert.

St Thomas's Cathedral – bearded clerical gentleman with shaven monk-like hair, and the ghost of Thomas Becket, sighted in 1927. Both apparitions were accompanied by the tinkling of bells.

Sally Port Hotel – ghost of the MI6 diver Buster Crabb, who spent his last night here before spying on a Russian vessel in Portsmouth Harbour and disappearing in 1956.

Southsea Castle – ghost of lighthouse keeper's daughter, who died of scarlet fever. Her ghost is reported to have selected an appropriately scarlet-coloured dress from her wardrobe.

Wymering Manor – said to be Hampshire's most haunted house, with eighteen ghosts to choose from, including a nun with bloody hands, the ghost of Jane Austen's brother, and a randy knight called Reckless Rod who was impaled on a sword thrown by a very annoyed husband.

Portsmouth Music

Portsmouth has had a vibrant and lively music scene which continues to this day. Some of the city's notable past and current bands and musicians include:

Joe Jackson, who grew up in Paulsgrove. His first gig was as the frontman of a band at Cumberland Tavern, Eastney. Recorded demos at recording studio in London Road. Signed to A&M, first album Look Sharp! and first hit Is she really going out with him? charted on both sides of Atlantic.

Paul Jones, lead vocalist, harmonica player of Manfred Mann (1962-66), born in Portsmouth, in 1942. Attended Portsmouth Grammar School and was a cathedral chorister.
Wrote 5-4-3-2-1 for TV pop show *Ready, Steady Go!* Went solo, had hits before taking up acting and latterly radio presenting. Currently a member of The Blues Band and The Manfreds.

Brian Howe, former lead singer with rock band Bad Company (1986-1994), was born in Portsmouth in 1953. He replaced Paul Rodgers when the band reformed in 1986. They had nine chart hits in USA, including two number ones.

Nicky Wire of Welsh rock band Manic Street Preachers attended Portsmouth Polytechnic in the late 1980s, but completed a degree in Political History at the University of Wales.

Brian Eno, musician, composer, played clarinet in the Portsmouth Sinfonia, produced their first two albums. Member of Roxy Music, later pioneer of ambient music.

Roger Hodgson, songwriter, vocalist, musician of Supertramp, born in Portsmouth, in 1950, son of a naval officer. Brought up in Oxford. Co-founded band, 1969. Writer of most of their hits which feature his distinctive high-pitched voice, including The Logical Song, Dreamer, Give a Little Bit and Breakfast in America.

Simon Dupree and the Big Sound formed in Porstmouth by Derek, Phil, and Ray Shulman, with Peter O'Flaherty, Eric Hine and Tony Ransley. Their biggest hit was with psychedelic Kites (1967). The Shulmans later formed prog rock group Gentle Giant.

Dillie Keane, founder member of cabaret trio Fascinating Aida, born in Southsea, in 1952.

Mick Jones, co-founder of band Foreigner, born in Portsmouth, in 1944. Was member of Spooky Tooth, wrote Foreigner's most successful single, I Want to Know What Love Is (1984).

Luke Haines, leader of The Auteurs, says he learned guitar in 'the red light district of Portsmouth'. Brought up in the city, formally trained as a musician, and almost won Mercury Prize, in 1993.

Roland Orzabel of Tears for Fears born Portsmouth, 1961. His family moved to Bath when he was a baby. He was the main song writer and vocalist and wrote many hits, including Mad World.

Nicky Wire of Welsh rock band Manic Street Preachers attended Portsmouth Polytechnic in the late 1980s, but completed a degree in Political History at University of Wales.

Julia Fordham, singer-song writer, was born prematurely in front room of family home, Portsmouth, in 1962. Career started in the early 1980s as backing singer for Mari Wilson and Kim Wilde. Has had several hits including Happy Ever After.

Murray Gold, born in Portsmouth, in 1969, educated Portsmouth Grammar School. Composer for stage, film and TV. Credits include *Doctor Who* and *Shameless*. Also dramatist; radio play *Kafka the Musical* (2011) starred David Tennant.

Richard Harwood, award-winning cellist, born in Portsmouth, in 1979. He made a Radio 3 debut at the age of thirteen, performing the Elgar *Concerto*.

Hixxy, UK DJ and musician, born Ian Hicks, Portsmouth, 1975. DJ career began with song Toytown which was a top-ten hit in 1996.

Ben Falinski, Ivyrise frontman, grew up in Cosham. The band, which has supported Bon Jovi, had two hits in the BBC Radio One Independent Chart, and released their debut album in 2011.

Portsmouth Music Today

Ten of the **best emerging bands and musicians** of the local scene are:

The Strange Death of Liberal England, perhaps the best known band from Portsmouth in recent years. Their music is 'about wars, graves and solitude' with 'thudding pianos, growling basslines, and relentless percussion' (The *Guardian*).

Bemis popular acoustic rockers, who can sell out a gig on word of mouth alone.

Huw Olesker has a burgeoning career both solo and with his band **The Barebackers**.

Attack! Vipers! play hardcore the way it should be played, fast and loud.

Andrew Foster is at the forefront of the singer-songwriter scene in Portsmoth and beyond.

Joe Black blends an old-school vaudeville persona with witty and macabre songs.

The Dawn Chorus is championed by acoustic-punk troubadour Frank Turner and has a stong fanbase.

The Boy I Used To Be have played far and wide, from launch parties for Channel 4's *Skins* to exclusive gigs in London.

Becky Jerams is an accomplished performer of pop ballads and rock, but is best known as a writer: one of her songs, La La Love, features in a Mandy Moore movie.

The Visitors' music was included on demo models of the Playstation 3 on its high profile release, and when Sony launched a video-streaming programme for the console, this band has featured.

Festivals and Venues

Both the The King's Theatre and The New Theatre Royal offer a varied and exciting programme that includes drama, comedy, opera, dance and live music.

The Portsmouth Guildhall is the city's biggest venue, and attracts top acts, bands, stand-ups and clairvoyants.

The Wedgewood Rooms in Albert Road has a reputation as a cutting-edge live music, comedy and alternative club venue. It attracts the up-and-coming bands of the future and established top names alike.

The Cellars at Eastney, a converted pub opposite the main entrance of the former Royal Marine barracks, is possibly the most intimate live music and comedy venue in the country, but punches well above its weight with an eclectic programme of big names and quality up-and-coming acts.

The Jolly Sailor on Clarence Parade has regular live entertainment.

Southsea Bandstand in West Battery Gardens, neighbouring Southsea Castle, offers a programme of free Sunday afternoon concerts every summer, appealing to all ages and tastes.

The Portsmouth Festivities is one of the major cultural events in the city, an annual arts festival that takes place over eleven days in June, featuring professional artists, performers and speakers of international renown.

The Heavy Horse Weekend is held over the spring bank holiday in Castle Field and offers a taste of the countryside by the sea. The activities end with an impressive Heavy Horse Parade on Monday.

The Portsmouth International Kite Festival, one of the country's premier kite-flying events, is held on Southsea Common annually, over a weekend in late August, attracting thousands of spectators.

The Victorian Festival of Christmas takes place at the Historic Dockyard.

Portsmouth Multicultural Festival is held on Castle Field at the beginning of September and the green Portsmouth

Summer Fair in Victoria Park in June. Look out for other advertised events on Southsea Common, Gunwharf Quays, the Historic Dockyard and Guildhall Square.

Pompey Pubs Past and Present

A selection of historic Portsmouth pub names (1716 to date), tells a timeless tale:

Roving Sailor (Bath Square); The Magnet (Greetham Street, Landport); The Sailor's Welcome (Queen Street, Portsea); The Hand-in-Hand (St George's Square, Portsea); The Sailor's Arms (Commercial Road, Landport); The Invitation (Prince Frederick Place, Southsea); The Land of Promise (London Road, Landport); The Cock (Portsmouth Common, Kingston); The Hampton (Hampton Street); The Rising Sun (Buckland Street, Buckland); The Majestic (Victoria Street, Landport); The Glorious Apollo (Gunwharf Road, Old Portsmouth); The Bush Hotel (King's Road, Southsea); The Spread Eagle (Arundel Street); The Fawcett Inn (Fawcett Road); The Maidenhead (High Street, Old Portsmouth); The Union (Fratton Road); The Locomotive Tavern (Railway View, Landport); The Tally Ho (Nile Street, Landport); The Fountain Inn (Warblington Street, Old Portsmouth); Mighty Fine (Commercial Road); The Still (Kent Street, Portsea); The Surprise (Baker Street, Landport); The Phoenix (Torrington Road, North End); Sailor's Return (Unicorn Street, Portsea);The Slip Inn (Bishop Street, Portsea); The Steam Reserve (Havant Street, Portsea); The Invincible (Wickham Street, Portsea); The Fountain Inn (London Road, Landport); The Registry (St Michael's Road, Landport).

As the country's premier naval port, and a garrison town, pubs and breweries have played a big part in the city's economic and social history. In 1869, there were an astonishing 897 licensed pubs and beerhouses in Portsmouth. Today, the city has a diminishing number, but many old pubs with character survive, catering for all tastes.

For a good view: The Still and West in Bath Square offers superb views of busy Portsmouth Harbour. The Churchillian on Portsdown Hill provides panoramic views of Portsea Island. The Dolphin pub in the High Street (opposite the Cathedral) is one of the oldest in the city, dating from the seventeenth century. There are also thirty cosmopolitan pubs and restaurants at Gunwharf Quays.

For good beer: The Hole in the Wall in Great Southsea Street; The Leopold Tavern, Albert Road, Southsea; The Florence Arms, Florence Road, Southsea; The Sir Loin of Beef, Highland Road, Southsea; The Winchester Arms, Winchester Road, Buckland; The Barley Mow, Castle Road, Southsea are all highly rated.

City Weathervanes

Look up at the rooftops while walking the streets of the city and you will see a wealth of fascinating architectural detail, including a wide diversity of chimney pots, cupolas and spires. As an island town, weathervanes had a practical function, and each one is unique.

Left to right:

Branksmere House, Queen's Crescent Southsea, built for the Brickwood brewery family in 1895 (private house).

Civic pride finds expression on top of a flagpole in Victoria Park where the municipal star and crescent smile down, presumably with the message 'Heaven's wind our guide'.

Ship flying on the former Municipal College, now part of the University, in King Henry I Street.

Bewitched private house in Southsea.

Golden Cock on the Royal Garrison Church, Old Portsmouth.

Golden barque, a replica of the gilt copper original, dated 1710, blown down in the 1950s and now preserved inside the Cathedral.

The brush of a running fox points downwind in the unlikely setting of Portsmouth Dockyard.

Futuristic design from the 1930s on the Manor House pub in Drayton.

Gunwharf Quays' Gate vane bearing the negative image of three torpedoes, erected when HMS *Vernon* became a shore base in 1923.

Lost bearings at the former Royal Marine Barracks at Eastney.

Queen Alexandra Hospital, *c.* 1908.

Restored clocktower, cupola and vane of the Georgian Storehouse No. 10 in the Historic Dockyard – the vane was rescued from the rubble after wartime bombing.

Stylised Cock on Thomas Ellis Owen's St Jude's Church, Southsea.

Pegasus rising into the sea breeze at Beach Tower, Southsea.

Castle in the air on the former Castle Street premises of Flemings.

Not a Lot of People Know That ...

Prime Minister William Pitt the Elder was decapitated in a freak accident in Portsmouth in the nineteenth century. A violent gale blew in a window of the Queen's Room in Portsea and shards of lethal glass sliced through his neck. Mr Allsop, who owned the waxwork collection, was not best pleased.

In the 1950s, Southsea was proud of and famed for its illuminations, which turned the seafront into a 'fairyland' of cartoons depicted in multi-coloured light bulbs. In 1954, they included a dog smoking a cigarette.

Portsmouth-born PM 'Sunny Jim' Callaghan never said 'Crisis? What Crisis?' in the late 1970s. It was made up by the *Sun*, the phrase having been taken from Portsmouth-born Roger Hodgson's band Supertramp's album of that title.

The Artillery Barracks in Broad Street was the site of the last ever official flogging of a British soldier (as opposed to whipping, which wasn't abolished until 1948).

The phrase *pour encourager les autres* has local, fictional origins. Voltaire satirised the execution (in Portsmouth Harbour) of Admiral Byng in *Candide* (1759). Candide is so shocked by the spectacle that he refuses to disembark.

In 1899, James Higgins, aged sixty-eight, was charged with mutilating a copy of the *Portsmouth Times* at the Public Library, 'doing damage to the amount of one penny'.

In 2003, Tate art gallery experts discovered that two Turner paintings of Venice were actually of Portsmouth.

Rat Island in Portsmouth Harbour is said to have acquired the name in the nineteenth century. The rats gathered there to gorge themselves on discarded washed-up entrails from the abbatoir of nearby Royal Clarence Victualling Yard.

A fish was landed at Portsmouth in 1870 with a champagne bottle in its stomach. Throw in some chips and you've got all the ingredients of a good night in.

What's in a Name?

In 1860, a man got out of his bath and stood at his window in Penny Street 'wearing only his spectacles'. Magistrates found him guilty of indecent exposure and sentenced him to one month's imprisonment with hard labour. His name was Mr Little.

In the early nineteenth century, a tobacco pipe manufacturer working in St George's Square was named Mr Clay.

Pompey's most well-known fan changed his name in 1994, by deed poll to John Portsmouth Football Club Westwood (*see* picture p.96).

In the late 1880s, a Mr Careless of Arundel Street was working as a 'bird stuffer'.

The landlady of the Golden Bell pub in St Mary's Street in the early nineteenth century was a Maria Bacchus. (Bacchus is the Roman god of wine and intoxication.)

A local clergyman, opposed to the 1843 Factories Bill which was intended to provide education to poor children in industrial areas, was the Revd Bastard.

A brothel run by two women in Ashburton Road was raided by police during the First World War. The police found 'evidences of what had been transpiring' and a man hiding. The two women had been observed entertaining servicemen over a number of days. The arresting officer was a Detective Sergeant Hoare.

Another brothel, operating in the 1860s, was located in Nobbs Lane.

In 1705, there were 228 men on the Portsmouth electoral roll. Amongst them were a Mr Cockwell, a Mr Sheath and a Mr Fucke. That's quite enough of that sort of thing.

Plague, Pestilence and War

The *Mary Rose* was built in Portsmouth in 1509-11, and was named after Henry VIII's favourite sister. On 19 July 1545, she led the fleet out of harbour to engage advancing French galleys but came under fire and turned to fire broadside guns and wait for support. A gust of wind is said to have forced her over. As her low gun-ports were open she quickly filled and sank. All but around thirty-five of a crew of 400 survived.

The Plague of 1563 killed around a third of the town's population. Bodies were buried hastily at night by men who were 'either brave or drunk, or both'. During the Great Plague of 1665/66, the gravediggers buried fifteen corpses a day. Graves were left so shallow that they were covered with crows and ravens.

The *Royal George* was being repaired at Spithead on 29 August 1782. The ship was low in the water because of the added weight of 600 visitors – wives, children, moneylenders and prostitutes – and water was lapping close to gun ports. A sudden breeze apparently forced her over, water poured in and she sank in an instant. Around 1,000 crewmen died, together with up to 300 women and sixty children. Bodies resurfaced for several days afterwards and watermen tied ropes around their ankles and towed them ashore.

In 1846, a local doctor, lamenting the lack of sewers, warned that 'the island of Portsea is one large cesspool' and that well-water was at serious risk. Two years later an outbreak of cholera killed 152 residents, many of them children, and the following year a further 800. It wasn't until 1863 that a proper sewerage system began to be put in place.

The Battle of Jutland resulted in the loss of 6,097 men, the majority from the Portsmouth area. Some mothers received several telegrams at once, with sons and fathers serving and dying together on the same ship. It was said that there were forty widows living in one street.

The Blitz – during the Second World War there were 1,581 air-raid warnings sounded in the city and sixty-seven air raids. A total of 930 civilians were killed, with 2,837 injured. Nearly 7,000 houses were destroyed and an equal number seriously damaged. A total of 1,320 high-explosive bombs, thirty-eight parachute (land) mines and over 40,000 incendiaries fell on the city, making it 'the most battered city in the country outside of London'.

Portsmouth Omens

On a visit in 1729, S. Martin Leake described Portsmouth Point as Gomorrah, pairing it with the notorious Gallows Point in Jamaica, which had a reputation for being like Sodom. The Jamaican port had been destroyed by an earthquake in 1692, and many people believed it to be divine retribution. Twenty-one years after Leake's visit, Portsmouth was hit by an earthquake. The few houses that were slightly damaged suggest an act of divine irritation.

There was a popular belief that if ever the bust of King Charles I was removed from its mount in the wall of the Square Tower, then grave misfortune would fall upon Portsmouth. In 1937, the bust was taken down and loaned for display in a Royal Academy exhibition. Within four years, much of the city was in ruins.

According to the groups 'Proles for Modernism' and the 'Equi-Phallic Alliance', the Tricorn was built on a Neolithic ritual landscape, which became a Druid place of worship, protected by 'an apple goddess St Margaret of Antioch'. The groups believed that the destruction of the Tricorn would lead to the destruction of Portsmouth. The Tricorn was demolished in 2004 …

After his travels through all France into
Spain, and having paſſed very many
dangers both by ſea and land he arrived
here the 5ᵗʰ day of October 1623.

Things to do in Portsmouth – Checklist

Eat fish and chips on the seafront – the smell of hot vinegar and sound of the surf. ☐

Have a putt on the green at Eastern Parade, and then sit down with a generous slice of the famous cake served at the Tenth Hole café. ☐

Stroll along the Millennium walkway and take in the historic sites en route. Look for the paving with the chain links pattern, and follow. ☐

Stand on the bow of the *Victory*, stretch out your arms and pretend you're Kate or Leo. ☐

How about a day of tacky pleasures on Clarence Pier: ice-cream, arcades and thrilling rides for the kids. ☐

Dare your children to stand on the glass floor at the top of the Spinnaker Tower. ☐

Walk the ramparts at Old Portsmouth overlooking the Solent and imagine the magnificent fleet reviews of the past. ☐

If you think ships, 'seen one, seen 'em all', a day at the Historic Dockyard will make you think again. ☐

Quaff a pint or two at one of Portsmouth's real-ale pubs. ☐

Take an evening stroll along Albert Road and breathe in the aromatic spices and herbs of the world's cuisine that wafts out into the fresh night air from the restaurants. ☐

An *al fresco* picnic, free music and the waters of the Solent as a backdrop; you can't beat Southsea Bandstand on a lazy Sunday afternoon. ☐

Dig your toe into the briney on Southsea beach and make out that you've swum the Channel. ☐

Climb the keep at Portchester Castle, look out over the harbour and blow the cobwebs away. ☐

Websites

www.actionstations.org

www.aspex.org.uk

www.charlesdickensbirthplace.co.uk

www.ddaymuseum.co.uk

www.english-heritage.org.uk

www.explosion.org.uk

www.history.inportsmouth.co.uk.

www.historicdockyard.co.uk

www.hms-victory.com

www.hmswarrior.org

www.maryrose.org

www.memorials.inportsmouth.co.uk

www.portsmouthcitymuseums.co.uk

www.portsmouthmuseums.co.uk

www.portsmouthnaturalhistory.co.uk

www.portsmouthpubs.org.uk

www.royalarmouries.org

www.royalmarinesmuseum.co.uk

www.royalnavalmuseum.org

www.submarine-museum.co.uk

www.southseacastle.co.uk

www.spinnakertower.co.uk

www.visitportsmouth.co.uk

Captions and permissions:

Thanks to Portsmouth Libraries; University of Portsmouth; Hampshire Constabulary; *The News*; Graham Hurley; Stephen Weeks; Chris Owen; Tim Reynolds; Karen Sadden; Parves Khan; Killian Walsh; Debbie Button; Ellie Stokes; Drusilla Moody; Louise Rodwell; Tim Backhouse; Gilli Kennedy; James Daly; Gemma Gray; Mike Taylor; Dave Allen; Jo Godfree; John PFC Westwood; Keela of The Hole in the Wall; Portsmouth City Council (PCC); United States Government (USG); Portsmouth Grammar School (PGS).Other images are by the author or are in the public domain. Special thanks to Matt Merritt for p. 106.

Page: